YOU CHOOSE
BOOKS

THE INTERNATIONAL
SPACE STATION

An Interactive Space Exploration Adventure

by Allison Lassieur

Consultant:
Richard Bell, PhD
Associate Professor of History
University of Maryland, College Park, Maryland, USA

Raintree is an imprint of Capstone Global Library Limited, a company incorporated in England and Wales having its registered office at 264 Banbury Road, Oxford, OX2 7DY – Registered company number: 6695582

www.raintree.co.uk
myorders@raintree.co.uk

Editor: Adrian Vigliano
Designer: Kayla Rossow
Media Researcher: Wanda Winch
Production Specialist: Laura Manthe

ISBN 978-1-4747-1100-5 (paperback)
20 19 18 17 16
10 9 8 7 6 5 4 3 2 1

British Library Cataloguing in Publication Data
A full catalogue record for this book is available from the British Library.

Acknowledgements
We would like to thank the following for permission to reproduce photographs: NASA, cover, 10, 12, ESA/Hubble Heritage Team (STScI/AURA), nebula design, Johnson Space Center, 14, 20, 23, 29, 35, 40, 51, 57, 60, 62, 67, 70, 72, 76, 80, 85, 88, 96, 100, 105, Kennedy Space Center, 46, Marshall Space Flight Center, 42, 44, Marshall Space Flight Center/Chesley Bonestell, 6; Shutterstock: HelenField, lunar surface design, HorenkO, paper design

Every effort has been made to contact copyright holders of material reproduced in this book. Any omissions will be rectified in subsequent printings if notice is given to the publisher.

All the internet addresses (URLs) given in this book were valid at the time of going to press. However, due to the dynamic nature of the internet, some addresses may have changed, or sites may have changed or ceased to exist since publication. While the author and publisher regret any inconvenience this may cause readers, no responsibility for any such changes can be accepted by either the author or the publisher.

Printed and bound in China.

Contents

ABOUT YOUR ADVENTURE

The International Space Station is one of the world's most ambitious engineering marvels. It took an army of designers, engineers, scientists and astronauts around the globe to make the science fiction of a station in space come true.

In this book you'll explore how the choices people made meant the difference between success and failure. The events you'll experience happened to real people.

Chapter One sets the scene. Then you choose which path to read. Follow the directions at the bottom of each page. The choices you make will change your outcome. After you finish your path, go back and read the others for new perspectives and more adventures.

YOU CHOOSE the path
you take through history.

Space stations like the one engineer Wernher von Braun imagined in 1952 helped ignite public interest in this new area of space exploration.

SCIENCE FICTION COMES TO LIFE

The idea of a permanent station in space where people could live used to be nothing more than science fiction. In 1869, a story called "The Brick Moon", by Edward Everett Hale, described a round brick structure launched into orbit with people on board. The "brick moon" was the first description of a space station. After that, writers and scientists imagined round space stations, flat space stations, tube-shaped space stations and even an inflatable space station!

Turn the page.

Then in the 1950s, another science fiction idea did become real: space flight. The Soviet Union put the first satellite, *Sputnik I*, into space in 1957. Four years later, in 1961, Soviet cosmonaut Yuri Gagarin became the first human to see Earth from space. In 1969, the world watched as humans walked on the Moon. Suddenly the idea of a permanent station in space didn't seem so much like fiction after all.

The first try at a real space station came in the 1970s. The Soviet Union launched the experimental Salyut 1 space station in 1971. It stayed in orbit for 175 days. One three-man crew stayed on the station for three weeks. In 1973 the United States sent the Skylab station into orbit. It stayed in space for six years. During that time, Skylab had three crews, and each crew lived in space for up to several months.

Both were designed to test systems that a permanent station would need. Eventually they were both shut down and sent crashing to Earth. But they proved that a permanent station could be a reality.

In 1984 President Ronald Reagan announced that the United States would build the first permanent space station. Reagan said: "A space station will permit quantum leaps in our research in science, communications and in metals and lifesaving medicines which could be manufactured only in space." Then he challenged other countries to join the United States in this adventure, saying: "We want our friends to help us meet these challenges and share in their benefits. NASA will invite other countries to participate so we can strengthen peace, build prosperity and expand freedom for all who share our goals."

Turn the page.

Eventually the leaders of space programmes in Russia, Europe, Japan, Brazil and Canada joined the project. In 1998 the first section of the International Space Station (ISS) was launched into orbit. Since 2000 the ISS has orbited Earth, welcoming astronauts from all over the world to live and work there.

Skylab helped pave the way for the ISS.

The ISS represents the first time that a global team of engineers and scientists combined forces to design and create a space station. But why build it in the first place? The ISS exists to be a laboratory and to study how humans can live in space. Every part of the ISS was engineered and designed to answer important science questions.

You've always been excited by the idea of space exploration. Almost from the first time you looked up at the night sky you've dreamed of learning everything you can about space. Space jobs are difficult, and some can be dangerous. But you're ready to make a difference exploring the universe.

To be a systems engineer and design the robotics, life support and other systems on the ISS, turn to page 13.
To fly to the station as a shuttle astronaut, delivering and installing modules (sections) during ISS construction, turn to page 47.
To be an astronaut living on the station, turn to page 73.

The launch of the space shuttle *Columbia* on
12 April 1981 opened the door to a new era
of possibilities in space exploration.

CHAPTER 2

ENGINEERING THE IMPOSSIBLE

You've always been excited by space travel. At first you wanted to be an astronaut. But it was the spaceships themselves that you loved more. Eventually you realized that you wanted to design and build spacecraft. You went to college and learned to be an engineer who designs and builds machines.

While you were in school in the mid-1990s, you watched with great interest as the Space Shuttle programme was in full swing. This NASA programme built reusable shuttles and sent astronauts into orbit.

13

At first your ambition is to work on the shuttle programme. Then you hear that work has started on the new ISS. You've studied the engineering designs of earlier space stations like Skylab and Salyut in class, but the ISS is going to be even better. Suddenly your dream gets bigger – to help design systems on the ISS.

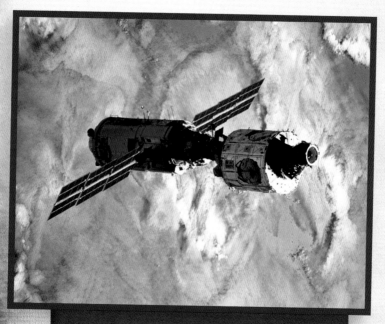

The space shuttle *Endeavour* crew connected the first ISS module, Zarya (left), with the second piece, Unity (right) on 6 December 1998.

The first section of the ISS is a Russian-made module called Zarya, or "dawn". It is sent into orbit in 1998 and will provide the initial power for the ISS. NASA's goal is to build and install communications, life support and other components of the ISS in four years. All of the partner countries, including Canada, Japan, Russia and the European Space Agency (ESA), will be designing and building different parts of the ISS.

You graduate at exactly the right time. Engineering design companies working on the ISS around the world are looking for new talent. To your delight, you get a job with one of them! You're only one engineer on this huge project, but you can't wait to make your mark in space.

To join the team that will design a robotic arm for the Canadian Space Agency (CSA), turn to page 16.
To be part of the U.S. team that will design the environmental and life support systems, turn to page 24.

On your first day, the boss gathers all the new engineers together. "One of the Canadian Space Agency's (CSA) contributions to the ISS will be a robotic arm," he begins. "The CSA developed its first arm, called Canadarm, for the space shuttles. The CSA's job now is to create the next generation of the Canadarm," the boss continues. "The arm for the ISS must be bigger and better, so the CSA has hired our engineering company to do it."

"Here's what we need," your boss tells the group. "The whole station will be built in space, and the American space shuttles will take it up into space one section at a time. This robotic arm will have to be one of the first things in orbit, because it will be needed to unload and move all the rest of the parts when they arrive."

You know that every shuttle has its own robotic arm. Each arm can only reach about 15 metres (49 feet). Each has six joints that allow it to rotate and move. "But the shuttle arm doesn't have the mobility or the strength to build a whole space station," your boss continues, as if he had read your mind. "The arm of the ISS has to be much bigger, better and have more movement."

The engineers will be divided into two groups. One will come up with ideas for how the arm will have more freedom of movement outside the station. The other team will work on how the astronauts will control the arm from inside the station. You like the idea of coming up with designs that will help such a big piece of machinery move smoothly. But working with astronauts sounds great too.

To be on the outside movement team, turn to page page 18.
To be on the arm-control team, turn to page 20.

The ISS will only have one robotic arm. It has got to be able to rotate and to move up, down and sideways. It has to be strong enough to control huge payloads. It also has to be delicate enough to move things without doing any damage.

How will one arm reach every part of the station? For days your team struggles to come up with ideas. Idea after idea is thrown out. It seems impossible.

One day you're sitting outside eating lunch, and notice a tiny caterpillar crawling along. Suddenly you get an idea!

"We can make the arm move like a caterpillar," you explain excitedly to the team. You show them how the arm could have a special latch on each end. "The surface of the space station will have grappling fixtures in several places. The arm could move like a caterpillar, going end over end, from fixture to fixture. That would allow it to move all over the station's surface."

Everyone loves the idea. But there are still lots of questions about how it will work. The latches you imagine are something no one has ever seen before. The grappling fixtures are new, too. Each component will take a lot of time and thought to create. But both are vital for your idea to work.

To design the latches on the end of the arm, turn to page 37.
To design the grappling fixtures, turn to page 39.

19

The robotic arm has to be controlled from inside the space station. The astronauts need a workstation where they can operate the arm. Your team has rules to follow while designing the workstation. The controls need to be easy to understand. If there's a problem, the astronaut needs to be able to fix it fast. The astronauts will use computers to move the arm, but they also must have some kind of manual control.

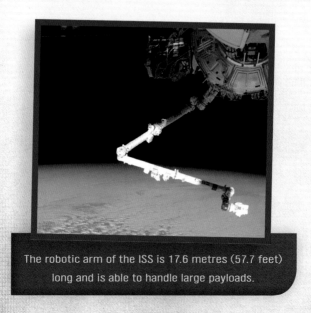

The robotic arm of the ISS is 17.6 metres (57.7 feet) long and is able to handle large payloads.

To work on the workstation computer design, go to page 21.
To work on the manual control design, turn to page 22.

"There isn't much room inside the space station for a lot of bulky hardware," you explain to the team. "The computers have to be small but powerful." The solution is to use portable computers, similar to laptops. Three monitors line up above the computers. Cameras mounted outside send video to the monitors so the astronauts can see what the arm is doing. The design includes a panel of buttons and switches that control the cameras.

It's a good idea to have a video feed into the control area, so the astronauts can watch the arm as they move it. "We don't want the arm smashing into anything," you say.

It takes months to fine tune the design so everyone is happy. Once the computer and camera control design is done, the team gathers to put the computer controls and the manual controls together.

Turn to page 41.

The robotic arm will be able to move in many directions. The joints can move up and down, grab objects and "walk" along the station. It will grab and move payloads to different places. The arm needs to rotate and spin, too.

You start thinking about video games. "How about a joystick?" you ask during one meeting. "Like the ones we use to play games." Excitedly you sketch out the idea of a simple joystick. It moves the arm at angles. When you draw a trigger, everyone laughs.

"Is that for blasting aliens?" someone asks. You smile.

"No, when you pull the trigger the arm grabs the payload."

The team decides on two joysticks. A second joystick controls the up, down and sideways motion of the arm. Once the design is finished, the team meets with the rest of the group to put all the controls together.

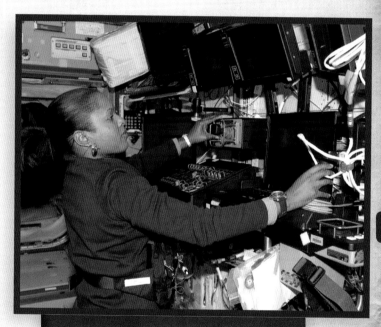

Astronaut Joan Higginbotham controls the robotic arm from the workstation on the ISS.

23

Turn to page 41.

You can't believe you're here, at your first job, and you'll be working on the ISS. You're the only new engineer on the team, but everyone makes you feel welcome. You're all waiting for a meeting to begin.

Dan Goldin, the head of the National Aeronautics and Space Administration (NASA), addresses your team. "How will the astronauts live in space?" he asks your group. Before anyone can answer, he continues, "That is the question your team has to answer."

"In the early days of the space programme," he says, "oxygen and water were carried into space in tanks. But that won't work for the International Space Station. People will be living there for weeks, or months. That's too long to rely on bringing enough oxygen and water from Earth. So the life support systems must use recycling and reusing technology."

At his suggestion, the engineers divide into two teams. One will work on the Oxygen Generation System. The other will work on the Water Recovery System. Both systems will work together to produce oxygen and water for the astronauts.

Each team will come up with ideas that will be the difference between life and death on the ISS. You're surprised at how nervous you feel, being responsible for such important designs. No matter which one you choose to work on, it will be up to you and the rest of the team to get everything right.

To design systems for clean air, turn to page 26.
To design systems for clean water, turn to page 32.

"As most of you know," your team leader begins, "the life support system needs for the ISS are vastly different than what the space shuttles needed. The space shuttles used a combination of oxygen and other chemicals brought from Earth and a system of built-in fans and filters for their air supply. That worked for short shuttle missions. But ISS astronauts will be in space for months, so the ISS air system must generate air for long periods of time."

"Each astronaut needs 0.84 kilograms (30 ounces) of oxygen per day to live," the team leader says. "So the air system must be able to maintain that level at all times."

"Why don't we use plants for oxygen?" you ask. "That's how it works on Earth. Plant life produces the oxygen that humans need to live."

The leader shakes her head. "It would take 300 to 500 plants per person to generate enough oxygen," she replied. "There's not enough room on the station for that many plants."

Clearly the team has to come up with another answer. "How about water?" someone asks. "Water is made up of two molecules, oxygen and hydrogen. Maybe there's a way to get oxygen out of water."

"That might work," the team leader says. "But will it generate enough oxygen? We might need backup systems, too."

To keep working on the idea of getting oxygen out of water, turn to page 28.
To design backup oxygen systems, turn to page 29.

Your team begins brainstorming ideas. "The scientific process for splitting water into hydrogen and oxygen is called electrolysis," you begin. "In electrolysis, an electrical current can be passed through the water."

"Now all we have to do is design a machine for the space station that can do that!" one of your teammates says.

It takes weeks to come up with a design that can perform electrolysis. There are a couple of problems to consider. Where will the electricity come from? And what will you do with the hydrogen? Hydrogen is flammable, so it's not something you want to keep on a space station if you don't have to. There are so many new challenges to tackle that each team member chooses one to focus on.

To work on the hydrogen problem, turn to page 31.
To work on the electricity problem, turn to page 42.

28

Your team comes up with two ideas for backup systems. One is a special pressurized tank with an airlock. The space shuttle brings containers of oxygen to the station and pumps the gas into these special pressurized tanks. But there are other gases in the air we breathe, such as nitrogen. So the design includes pumping nitrogen into other tanks.

You design a control that will mix the gases together in the same amounts as on Earth. Then the air can be pumped into the station for the astronauts to breathe safely.

Astronaut Carl Walz works on an oxygen generator on the ISS.

Turn the page.

The other idea is a system that makes oxygen with chemicals. You design special canisters that hold a mix of iron and sodium chlorate powder. If the astronauts need emergency oxygen, they put the canisters in a reactor. Then they pull a pin that ignites the chemicals inside the canister. The reaction of the burning chemicals creates oxygen.

The team likes these ideas, and one person calls the powder canisters "oxygen candles". One oxygen candle makes enough oxygen for one astronaut for one day.

It's time to meet up with the water team again.

Turn to page 44.

There isn't any question that the hydrogen has to go. It's far too dangerous. But how can it be removed from the ISS? One idea is to store it in canisters and take them off the station using a space shuttle. That creates more problems, though. It forces the space shuttle to carry cargo for which it might not have room. And putting the hydrogen in canisters is still dangerous. After days of design failures, you decide to take the problem to one of your teammates.

She thinks about the problem and you discuss solutions. "Maybe the gas could be vented off the station into space?" she says.

"That's a good idea," you say. The two of you design a venting system that will remove the hydrogen and other impurities from the station.

Now it's time for the oxygen team to join the water team.

Turn to page 44.

"Do you know how much water each station crew member will use in a year?" the lead engineer asks when your team assembles. "Thousands of kilograms of water – per person!" When the ISS is operational, crews will bring water from Earth. The assembly missions will take bags of water up for storage. But bringing water from Earth isn't a permanent solution. Your team's job is to create a water recycling and purification system for the station.

"Why can't we use the same water systems that the space shuttles use?" you ask. You know that the shuttles get their water from fuel cells. The fuel cells make electricity for a shuttle's power system using oxygen and hydrogen gas. A byproduct of this chemical reaction is water.

"Fuel cells are fine for short flights but they won't make enough water for long space station missions," the lead engineer says. "We need to create a long-term system that will recycle as much waste water as possible."

"Before we can go forwards, though, we need some information," the lead engineer says. "We have to know how much waste water will be generated so we will know what we have to work with. I need volunteers to go to the space station testing facility and gather waste water data. The rest of you will stay here and work on the designs for the Water Processor Assembly."

To gather data on waste water, turn to page 34.
To work on the Water Processor Assembly, turn to page 36.

33

Before you can design a good recycling system, you have to know what kind of waste water will be recycled on the space station. You and the other two team members who volunteered for this job settle in to watch, listen and study the different ways astronauts use water.

The astronauts are training to be ISS crew members, so they go through everything they will do in a normal day in space. In one day, crew members washed their hands 11 times, took 6 full body washes, shaved 3 times and brushed their teeth 11 times. Sweat and breathing made almost 9.1 kilograms (20 pounds) of water a day. And urine made about 9 kilograms per day. Altogether, the crew made about 21.8 kilograms (48 pounds) of waste water each day.

You never thought this kind of stuff would be interesting, but you're fascinated by how much water one human can make, and use, in a day. You and the rest of the team study the astronauts for a week, comparing each day's notes. Finally you come up with solid information on exactly how much water you have to work with.

The lead engineer is impressed. "This is exactly what we needed. Good work." Now the waste water group needs to reassemble, so they can use your data to design the systems.

Astronaut Leland Melvin worked on upgrading the water processing equipment on the ISS during his 2009 mission.

Turn to page page 44.

The team comes up with some interesting engineering designs to recycle waste water. The system includes special filters that will catch and separate gases, dirt and solid materials like dust and hair in used water. Other parts of the system heat the waste water and pass it through filters and sensors. The clean water is then pumped into storage tanks, ready to use. You contribute a design for special sensors that check the purity of the recycled water. After weeks of testing, the team finally gets the system working. Everyone prepares to meet with the oxygen team to put the designs together.

Turn to page 44.

The latch design you come up with surprises everyone. The robotic arm is not permanently anchored to the space station. Instead, you design a Latching End Effector for each end. These latches lock into a special plug. These plugs would be distributed around the surface of the station. One end of the arm is latched down, and the other end can move freely. When it's time to move to another part of the station, the free end plugs into a different fixture and locks down. The other end disconnects from its plug and swings up to a new position. In this way, the arm can "walk" from plug to plug around the outside of the station.

Turn the page.

Even better, each latch end has a camera and lights, so the astronauts can see where the arm is moving.

It's a great engineering design, and soon it is approved. But it's just the beginning. For months your team works out the details of the design until it's exactly right. It takes another year for the arm to be constructed. You're thrilled to be invited to watch the first tests of the arm. It works perfectly!

On 19 April 2001, Canadarm2 climbs into space aboard the space shuttle *Endeavour*. Three days later Canadian astronaut Chris Hadfield installs it on the ISS. Your idea will be used on the space station for years to come.

THE END

To follow another path, turn to page 11.
To read the conclusion, turn to page 101.

The grappling fixtures, or plugs, must be carefully placed around the station's surface. They have to be close enough together so that the arm can reach one while being locked into another. They also have to be strong enough to hold the arm while it moves and works in space.

After weeks of work the design is done. The plugs are called Power Data Grapple Fixtures. Each is a large cylinder that works like an electrical outlet. The end of the robotic arm "plugs" into the grapple fixture on the station's surface. It then connects with camera, video and data feeds inside the fixture. The arm stays locked into the fixture until it's time to move to another section of the station. The design also has to be applied to any object that will be delivered to the space station, so the arm can "grab" the payload in space.

Turn the page.

This is only the first step. It will be months before your design is built and tested. It will be longer after that before they are installed onto the ISS. There's a lot of work ahead, but it only makes you more excited. You imagine what it will be like to watch Canadarm2 move on a NASA video feed, and know it's because of something you created. You're so proud to have designed a part of the space station.

Astronaut Chris Hadfield on a spacewalk during the 2001 Canadarm2 installation mission.

THE END

To follow another path, turn to page 11.
To read the conclusion, turn to page 101.

The workstation is compact, so all the controls must be together in a small space. Everything must be within arm's reach of the astronaut who is working the controls. The biggest problem now is how the astronauts will work at the station in zero gravity. They can't sit in regular chairs – they would float away! Together everyone comes up with a restraint system that holds the astronaut safely at the workstation. The joysticks are put on either side of the computer, so the astronaut can reach them easily. The entire workstation fits in a space the size of a small desk.

A few months later you and the team get to see a model of the workstation. It works beautifully! You can't wait for it to go up into the space station. Even though you will never go to space, your engineering designs will.

THE END

To follow another path, turn to page 11.
To read the conclusion, turn to page 101.

Your first thought is to design a battery of some kind. That would work, but it would need to be recharged. There must be another way. Where does the rest of the station's electricity come from? Solar panels! Maybe you can use the existing power grid of the station. You decide to run with this idea. After lots of hard work, you come up with a way for the electrolysis machine to pull electricity from the station's power.

Scientists and engineers at NASA's Marshall Space Flight Center in Alabama work to design and build life support systems for the ISS.

It works! Proudly you show it to the team, and they add it to the engineering design of the entire system. But it's only one problem solved. Each small part of the life support system is a new challenge that requires new solutions. Weeks, then months, go by as the team builds on each successful design. Your tireless work earns you a promotion, which is exciting. But the pride you feel knowing that your designs will keep astronauts alive is even better.

THE END

To follow another path, turn to page 11.
To read the conclusion, turn to page 101.

Everyone is excited to be back together and to share what they've done. You and the other team members spend a few weeks comparing and refining your designs so that they work seamlessly together. The Water Recovery system will make water for the Oxygen Generation system. It's exactly the kind of engineering systems the space station needs. Once up and running, it will give the station crew up to 9.1 kilograms (20 pounds) of oxygen a day and recycle more than 90 per cent of their waste water.

The Environmental Control and Life Support System (ECLSS) is a powerful device that provides for the basic needs of ISS crews.

Put together, the entire Environmental Control and Life Support System (ECLSS) is about the size of three refrigerators. Before it goes aboard the ISS, though, it has to be tested. You're thrilled to be invited to observe some of the testing. The testing engineers troubleshoot each part of the system, coming up with every possible problem that could happen in space. They perform tests to fix any problem. As you watch your designs pass every test, you can't help but be proud that you helped to make the systems that will keep astronauts alive in space for months at a time.

THE END

To follow another path, turn to page 11.
To read the conclusion, turn to page 101.

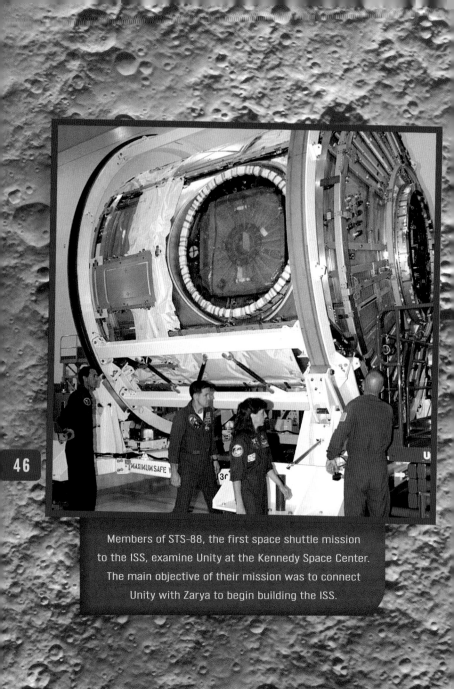

46

Members of STS-88, the first space shuttle mission
to the ISS, examine Unity at the Kennedy Space Center.
The main objective of their mission was to connect
Unity with Zarya to begin building the ISS.

CHAPTER 3

PUTTING IT TOGETHER

When people asked what you wanted to be when you grew up, you only had one answer: astronaut. You can hardly believe that your dream came true. You did become an astronaut. And you've been chosen as a space shuttle astronaut on the biggest mission ever: to help build the International Space Station.

One of the biggest engineering problems of the station is how to build it. It's too big to send up at once. That means it can't be built on Earth. Each piece will be designed and built on Earth, but the whole thing will be assembled in space.

47

Turn the page.

Your mission is to deliver the first large piece of the station up into space. It's the Destiny module, and it will be the laboratory on the station. The Destiny lab will be where astronauts conduct science experiments in the zero gravity of space.

You're confident that Destiny will work, but you can't be completely sure. Nothing that is going into the ISS can be tested in space before it's installed. But every piece has to work, in space, immediately. It's your job to make sure that it all runs smoothly. It's going to take many years to build the station. The world is counting on your team to get this right.

After the shuttle flight, you and the shuttle team arrive at the space station. Up to now, the space station has been in pieces. The first piece, Zarya, provided communications control and electrical power. After that, several other missions delivered supplies and more sections of the station. Just last year, in 2000, the first three-person station crew that would live and work on board went up. One person in that crew, William Shepherd, trained with you.

The Destiny module will nearly double the living and working space in the station. Right now it's in *Atlantis*'s cargo bay. Once the shuttle *Atlantis* docks, there will be a lot of work to do. The ISS crew is looking forward to seeing what you've brought from Earth, and they don't want to wait. But you also need to go over the attachment procedures.

To discuss Destiny's attachment procedures after docking, turn to page 50.

To unload supplies for the space station, turn to page 52.

The entire *Atlantis* crew, including Commander Kenneth Cockrell, pilot Mark Polansky, mission specialists Bob Curbeam, Tom Jones and Marsha Ivins, gather for a meeting. Everyone is excited, but tense. The Destiny module cost $1.38 billion. Every part of Destiny has been carefully engineered to work perfectly. There's no backup module. If anything goes wrong, there is no Plan B. You all understand the importance of getting everything right. The crew goes over the installation plan again and again. Ivins will use the robotic arm to lift Destiny out of the cargo bay. Curbeam and Jones will be outside, on a spacewalk, to help manoeuvre the module into place and secure it manually.

"I won't be able to see the module from where we are," Ivins says. "My only visuals will be the monitors inside the shuttle's flight deck." In some places, the clearance is only 7.5 centimetres (3 inches). You swallow hard. This is not going to be easy.

Ivins sees your face and laughs. "Don't worry. The entire galaxy is depending on it," she says. "No pressure!"

The ISS and *Atlantis* crews worked together to move Destiny out of the shuttle's cargo bay to begin the installation.

To volunteer to help Ivins with the robotic arm, turn to page 53.
To volunteer for a spacewalk with Curbeam and Jones, turn to page 55.

Commander Ken Cockrell safely docks the shuttle *Atlantis* with the station and connects the hatches. You get into your Extravehicular Mobility Unit (EMU), otherwise known as a spacesuit, and go through the procedure to open the hatches. It takes about two hours to make sure everything is ready to go. Then the hatches open and you greet the station crew.

Each shuttle mission brings supplies to the space station. The crew members have been here since November 2000, and it's February 2001 now. They are very happy to get the supplies you've brought – water bags, a spare computer, fresh food, power cables and DVD movies.

After a brief visit, the hatches are closed again. It's time to get the Destiny module ready for attachment.

To assist with using the robotic arm to lift Destiny, go to page 53.
To go on a spacewalk to attach the module from the outside, turn to page 55.

The shuttle's robotic arm is one of the most significant engineering successes in the space programme. No one had ever designed anything like it before. It was engineered to be lightweight, resistant to cold and heat and controlled by a joystick.

You have studied how the ISS robotic arm works but this is the first time you've seen it in action. Ivins explains what you've learned, including that it has six joints: two "shoulder" joints, one "elbow" joint and three "wrist" joints. She points to the joystick on the shuttle controls. "This controls the arm," she says. "I can move all the joints of the arm from here."

Turn the page.

The first job for the arm is to remove a docking tunnel. It's on the spot where Destiny will be attached to the station.

"Would you like to do this?" she asks. She reminds you that Mission Control on Earth monitors every robotic arm mission, to troubleshoot and provide support. But you'll be doing all the moving yourself.

You're itching to get your hands on the controls. But you didn't realize how enormous the arm was, or how precise the controller needs to be. One wrong move and that one-of-a-kind robotic arm could swing the wrong way, damaging something.

To work the robotic arm, turn to page 62.
To watch Ivins work instead, turn to page 64.

54

You, Jones and Curbeam are all in your spacesuits, waiting for the "go" to open the hatch and begin your spacewalk. It takes a few hours for Ivins to manoeuvre the module into place, and you wish you could watch. But there are no windows where you are waiting, so you talk to the other astronauts.

"If the hatch gets stuck, we're stuck," Jones says. He tells you that he was supposed to have taken his first space walk on another mission. But the handle to the hatch had stuck. They never got to leave the shuttle.

Would the hatch open this time? Yes! Everyone is smiling as they float into space.

Turn the page.

Everyone knows exactly what to do. You focus on connecting power, data and other life support cables that link Destiny to the space station. As you are connecting a cooling cable, something sprays out! This could be very dangerous. Immediately you realize that it's ammonia, one of the chemicals used as a coolant. You catch your breath for a second – a leak in a hose can be devastating. Not only could it compromise ISS systems, the chemical could damage your suit, which might kill you in space. Quickly you attach the cable and the leak stops.

You breathe again and check yourself. You don't see any chemicals on your suit. Thankfully it wasn't as bad as it could have been. You could continue your spacewalk. Or you could return to the shuttle to be on the safe side.

Most spacewalks last between five and eight hours, depending on the job the astronauts are trying to accomplish.

To continue the spacewalk, turn to page 58.
To return to the shuttle, turn to page 66.

You're trained to treat every accident as serious. Even though very little ammonia seems to have leaked, it's best to be careful. You stay outside for a full orbit around Earth to boil off any ammonia crystals that might have got on your suit. When it's time to return to the shuttle, Jones brushes you off to get rid of any more crystals. In the shuttle, everyone puts on oxygen masks. You wipe down your suits with wet towels. Quickly you realize that everything is alright.

The next day Destiny is finally locked down and secure. All the systems are hooked up and ready to go. It's time to step inside the new section of the space station for the first time.

Every part of the Destiny lab must be checked for any problems. It's your job to examine everything to make sure it's working properly.

To examine the laboratory racks, go to page 59.
To examine the space window, turn to page 67.

The engineers who designed Destiny made everything to fit in small spaces. Most of the systems were designed to fit on narrow racks. Each rack is about the size of a kitchen refrigerator. Destiny was made so that racks could be added, changed or replaced. Right now Destiny has five racks that hold the electric and life support systems. You examine them and they all are working properly.

Later, other shuttle missions will bring more racks up to the lab. Eventually Destiny will have at least 24 racks, which can hold more equipment and scientific experiments.

There is another spacewalk scheduled, and the astronauts could use your help installing equipment that will work with the robotic arm. Or you can continue inspecting the interior of the Destiny module.

To take another space walk, turn to page 60.
To continue the inspection, turn to page 67.

After the normal pre-spacewalk routines, you finally float into *Atlantis*'s cargo bay, along with Jones and Curbeam. It will take some time to carefully make your way to the area where you will work. In the meantime, inside the station Ivins manipulates the robotic arm to move a docking adaptor. The docking adaptor will become the new docking port for shuttle missions in the future. Ivins positions the docking adaptor and soon it is secured. By the time she is done, you are in position to start your job.

Astronaut Robert Curbeam moved materials between *Atlantis* and the ISS on a space walk in 2001.

The task is to install equipment that will be used by the station's new robotic arm, which will be delivered and installed on another mission. After your team completes that task, the spacewalking crew moves to another spot on the ISS to install an air vent. Then you have the job of installing handrails and wires for future spacewalkers to hang on to. The final task is to attach a base for the future robotic arm.

That's all you are supposed to do today, but you're ahead of schedule. You could go ahead and do some of tomorrow's jobs now. Or you can return to the station and help the space station crew activate systems in the new module.

To continue with the spacewalk, turn to page 69.
To go back inside the space station, turn to page 70.

You've trained for this, but it's the first time you've done it in space. Carefully you grip the joystick and stare at the monitors. Computer commands flash onto the screen. The computer will automatically loosen the outside bolts that hold the docking tunnel in place. Will it work? You don't realize you're holding your breath until the bolts begin to release. You and Ivins smile. It's working exactly the way it's supposed to.

Astronaut Marsha Ivins assisted spacewalks on the 2001 mission by carefully controlling the robot arm from the flight deck.

After a few minutes you hand the joystick back to Ivins. You've got some time before Destiny is locked on and you can continue your mission. For now, though, you move to the shuttle's window. Far below you can see the hazy surface of Earth, blue against the blackness of space. You'll be up here for a few more days, but you know you'll never get tired of this view.

THE END

To follow another path, turn to page 11.
To read the conclusion, turn to page 101.

Smiling, you shake your head. She takes the joystick. "The computer will automatically release the bolts," she says. "At least, that's what they're designed to do."

Suddenly the song "Please Release Me" is blasting in the cockpit! Commander Cockrell must have put the song on to play a joke on Ivins and Mission Control. You smile when you hear a voice from Mission Control on Earth say, "You and Marsha have second careers as DJ's when you get back!"

Slowly the spacewalkers remove the docking tunnel and place it in a storage area. Then Ivins carefully grabs Destiny with the robotic arm. Slowly she lifts it out of the shuttle cargo bay. It takes 30 minutes to lift the module a few metres.

Once it is out of the cargo bay, Ivins flips the module right side up. Then she slowly moves it into position. Automatic latches and bolts secure the module to the station.

Success! This part of the job is done. Now the spacewalkers begin work to attach the electric and coolant cables. Soon Destiny will be a permanent part of the ISS.

THE END

To follow another path, turn to page 11.
To read the conclusion, turn to page 101.

Even small accidents can be deadly. You have been trained to take every potential problem seriously, especially during a spacewalk. You return to the shuttle and decontaminate your suit. You have to be very careful, because one wrong move and any ammonia on your suit could contaminate the rest of the crew. Thankfully, there isn't any ammonia on your suit. But it was a close call. Everyone inside wears their oxygen masks for about 20 minutes, just in case the toxic ammonia got into the life support systems.

Mission Control checks in to see how things are and you assure them that everything is fine. Your spacewalk is over for now, but there will be more opportunities to go back out later in the mission.

THE END

To follow another path, turn to page 11.
To read the conclusion, turn to page 101.

Destiny's window is a round glass porthole, 50.8 centimetres (20 inches) in diameter. Engineers designed the window to be a "science" window. High quality photos and videos taken from the window will help scientists to study things like floods, wildfires, avalanches and weather on Earth.

Astronaut Ellen Ochoa looks through Destiny's porthole window on a 2002 ISS mission.

Turn the page.

The window has four layers. The outer layer is the debris pane, which protects from flying space junk. The two middle panes help maintain cabin pressure, similar to the windows on an aircraft. The inside layer is a removable scratch pane to protect the window from the inside. It even has its own heater, to keep condensation from forming and fogging up the window.

You grab your camera and snap pictures of Earth as it floats beneath the station. Soon you'll be on your way back home, but for now you're happy to enjoy this amazing view.

THE END

To follow another path, turn to page 11.
To read the conclusion, turn to page 101.

You all agree to keep going. The next few hours go by quickly as you connect computer and electrical cables and attach a protective shutter to Destiny's window. Finally, after almost seven hours in space, you, Curbeam and Jones climb back into the station's airlock. As you float back into the station, you take one look back. It's a view you'll never forget.

THE END

To follow another path, turn to page 11.
To read the conclusion, turn to page 101.

Jones and Curbeam decide to continue working outside, but you float into the airlock and close it behind you. Soon you're ready to join the space station crew. Two of the crew, Yuri Gidzenko and Sergei Krikalev, are Russian cosmonauts. You know the American astronaut Bill Shepherd. They're all glad to have your help.

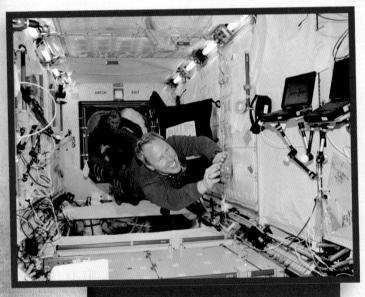

Astronauts Thomas Jones (front) and Kenneth Cockrell (back) float into Destiny to check out the newly installed laboratory.

The four of you go through the new module, turning on the atmosphere system that will help purify the station's atmosphere. Then you help adjust the carbon dioxide removal system in the living section. Everything works exactly as it is supposed to.

When the spacewalkers come back, all the hatches between the shuttle and the station are closed. This will conserve air. It also means the work day is over. Now the crew will have some time off to get ready for the last spacewalk tomorrow. You can relax with the rest of the crew.

THE END

To follow another path, turn to page 11.
To read the conclusion, turn to page 101.

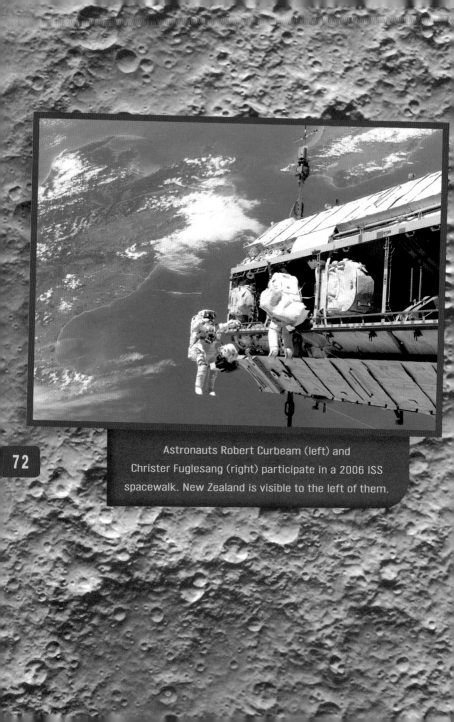

Astronauts Robert Curbeam (left) and
Christer Fuglesang (right) participate in a 2006 ISS
spacewalk. New Zealand is visible to the left of them.

CHAPTER 4

TO SPACE AND BEYOND

The International Space Station is as big as a football pitch and weighs more than 362.8 tonnes (400 tons). It has travelled more than 2.4 billion kilometres (1.5 billion miles) over 57,000 orbits around Earth. It's the brightest object in the night sky after the Moon. It flies at 28,164 kilometres (17,500 miles) per hour and orbits Earth once every 92 minutes. Everything on the station, from the bolts that hold it together to the food packaging, has been specially designed and engineered for space life.

Turn the page.

This engineering wonder has been fully operational since 2010, and it's now your home. You and two other astronauts, also called mission specialists, rode up to the space station in a shuttle. The three of you will join two Russian cosmonauts and a Japanese astronaut on this mission, or expedition, for six months. Each person has specific jobs to do while they're here. But there will also be time to relax, sleep and enjoy this once-in-a-lifetime experience.

Everyone starts the day in a tiny crew cabin with a sleeping bag attached to the wall. If you aren't attached to something you'll float away!

Some astronauts like to start their day with breakfast. Others like to wash first.

To wash, go to page 75.
To eat breakfast, turn to page 77.

There is no running water on the space station, because water can't flow in zero gravity. So the space station doesn't have any sinks or showers. Each crew member gets one packaged wet towel every two days. You'll also get two dry towels and two flannels a week, and packets of moist napkins every two days. It's not much, but astronauts don't get very dirty in space.

After wiping down with the wet cloth, it's time to brush your teeth. You picked your favourite toothpaste before you left Earth, and now you pull it out of a kit attached to the cabin wall. Drinking water comes in pouches, so you squeeze a drop onto your brush and watch it get sucked into the bristles. Then the toothpaste goes on, and into your mouth.

Turn the page.

Of course you can't spit in zero gravity. Well, you could, but it would get messy, fast. Instead, you take a mouthful of water, swish it around, and swallow everything, toothpaste and all. Now you're ready to start your day.

ISS crew members share a meal in the Unity section of the station in 2009.

To get some breakfast, go to page 77.
To start your duties, turn to page 78.

There isn't a kitchen on the station, but there is an eating area with a table. It's not like a table on Earth, though. This one is covered with straps and Velcro to keep food containers and napkins from floating away. And there are no chairs. Everyone floats around the table at mealtimes!

You eat everything out of packages that were specially engineered for the space station. They fit perfectly on the table, in the storage compartments and in the small warming oven that's used to heat food.

You choose scrambled eggs, apple juice and a fresh orange for breakfast. It's easy to heat up the scrambled eggs in the oven. Supply ships often bring fresh fruit to the space station, which is a nice treat. Once breakfast is over it's time to start your workday.

Turn to page 78.

Each astronaut has a to-do list every day. The space station is a research lab, filled with scientific experiments that need attention.

The space station is engineered so that all its systems work together, so if there's a problem in one spot it can affect many others. The crew has to check life support systems, update computer equipment and clean different parts of the station. You might also get new instructions from Mission Control if they notice something that needs to be done.

Today you have a list of duties inside the station. But Mission Control has just contacted the station. There is a broken pump outside that needs to be replaced. One of the cameras on the robotic arm also needs replacing. That means a spacewalk.

To prepare for a spacewalk, go to page 79.
To go through your other duties, turn to page 80.

It takes almost a day to get ready for a spacewalk. Every astronaut has a specific checklist to go through. The first thing to do is check your spacesuit, also known as an EMU. It's designed to keep you alive in space and every part of it must be in perfect working order. Especially important is the SAFER (Simplified Aid for EVA Rescue), which is a space life jacket. Normally you are tethered to the station by a cord so you don't float away. But if something happens and you do become detached, SAFER helps you get back to the station. It works like a jet pack, and you drive it with a joystick.

When the suit passes inspection you put it on and wait in the airlock. It takes a few hours to decompress before a spacewalk. When everything is ready, you open the hatch and float outside.

To replace the camera, turn to page 88.
To replace the pump, turn to page 91.

Today your main duties are to check and maintain some of the many scientific experiments on the space station. One item on the list catches your eye. As you read it, you smile. Often students from around the world send ideas for experiments in space. One group wanted to know if plants could grow in zero gravity.

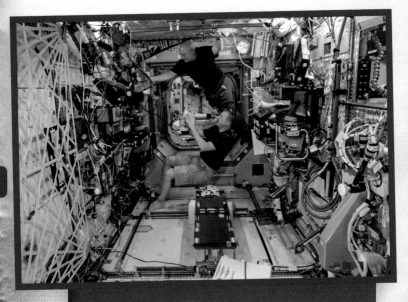

Astronauts Terry Virts (bottom) and Scott Kelly (top) work on a low-gravity-vision health experiment inside the Destiny laboratory in 2015.

You smile, thinking what a good question that is. Plants grow upwards towards the Sun, while their roots shoot downwards into the earth. What if a plant tried to grow where there is no "up" or "down"? You're impressed by the students who came up with this experiment.

Another experiment on the list sounds interesting too. Some scientists are conducting experiments on how the human body reacts to living in zero gravity. You already know that the human body does some interesting things in space. For instance, without the force of gravity pulling against the body, bones and muscles get weaker. Checking on either of these experiments would be interesting.

To work on the human body experiment, turn to page 82.
To check on the plants, turn to page 93.

Scientists want to know more about the effects of space life on a person. Also, astronauts must stay healthy in space. In space there isn't any gravity for muscles to work against. So muscles, including the heart, will lose strength. The only way to get any exercise is by going to the space gym. You check on this experiment by becoming a part of it.

Astronauts use exercise equipment that has been specially engineered for zero gravity. The stationary bike doesn't have a seat, because you can't sit down in zero gravity! Instead, the bike pedals have special clip-on shoes the astronaut wears to stay attached to the bike.

The treadmill looks normal except for big bungee cords attached to it. You put on a harness and clip the bungee cords to it. The cords keep you pulled down so you can run on the treadmill without floating away.

Before you start, you attach sensors to different parts of your body. The sensors will record your heart rate, blood pressure and other data. Scientists will use this data to study how space affects the body.

After your workout, there is one more job left to do. But Mission Control is calling. You can continue with your daily jobs and let another astronaut find out what's going on. Or you can see what Mission Control wants.

To find out what Mission Control wants, turn to page 84.
To go to your next space job, turn to page 95.

The news isn't good. A piece of space junk is on course to collide with the space station! There are more than 500,000 bits of orbital debris currently being tracked in space. Each one is flying around Earth at high speed. Mission Control tracks as much space debris as possible to make sure nothing gets too close to the space station. The piece of debris coming your way is about the size of a hand. It's probably part of an old satellite.

The crew discusses options with Mission Control. The only thing to do is to move the space station. If it changes orbit, the debris will miss it.

How do you move a gigantic space station? The station has thrusters on the Zvezda module section that can fire up and move the station. Also, the supply ship *Progress* that's docked at the station has its own rocket thrusters. They're strong enough to move the station, too.

The Zvezda module was the third piece of the ISS. It was connected to Zarya in July 2000.

To use *Progress*'s thrusters to move the station, turn to page 86.
To move the station using its own thrusters, turn to page 97.

The *Progress* cargo ship is able to move the station if needed. It's a good thing that it happens to be in dock right now, you think. Mission Control instructs the crew to close the hatches between the modules and to get into one of the two Russian *Soyuz* spacecraft, which are also docked. The *Soyuz* can be used as a "lifeboat" in case something happens to the station.

Once you're in the *Soyuz* there isn't anything to do but wait. You take your camera, hoping to get a few pictures of the space junk. But you don't see anything but black space. The debris must have zoomed by too far away to see.

Finally Mission Control says you can return to the station. Good thing, too, because you have to go to the toilet. But Mission Control says there's an incoming message from the president.

To go to the toilet first, go to page 87.
To listen to the message, turn to page 99.

Going to the toilet on the space station is not anything like going on Earth. Each piece of equipment is engineered to work in zero gravity.

One piece of equipment is a hose with a funnel attached to the top. Suction pulls liquid waste into bags that are thrown away later.

The station also is also equipped with a square toilet that looks like a camp toilet. But the hole is really small. Astronauts have to go through special training to use the space station toilet. The training toilet was fitted out with a camera at the bottom. You watched a video screen to practise getting your aim right.

You feel better now! If you're quick you will get back in time to hear the president's message.

Turn to page 99.

The cameras outside the space station take pictures of Earth and of the station itself. The cameras also help the astronauts see the robotic arm. One of the Earth-facing cameras is broken.

You use the handrails installed on the outside of the station to move to the camera. Your tools are tethered to your spacesuit so they won't float away. The job isn't too difficult but you take your time and make sure everything is done correctly.

The handrails on the outside of the ISS are the main tool astronauts use to move around on a spacewalk. Sometimes they may also hitch a ride on the robotic arm.

Suddenly you feel dizzy. It seems to be getting hot in your suit. Something must be wrong! You know it's common for astronauts to get space motion sickness. On Earth, your inner ear feels gravity and tells your brain which way is up and which way is down. But in space, without gravity, the inner ear can't tell what is "up" or "down". The brain gets confused trying to figure it out, and this causes dizziness. But this is the first time it's happened to you.

Instantly a voice from Mission Control comes in. They have been monitoring your vital signs, and spotted some trouble. They aren't sure what's wrong. It could be space motion sickness. You could be getting sick. You might have breathed in toxic fumes. Or something might have gone wrong with your spacesuit. You need to get back inside the station now.

Turn the page.

Breathing as normally as you can, you slowly make your way back to the air lock. The dizziness passes but this isn't a time to take chances. You're trained to take even the smallest physical change seriously. The hatch opens and you gratefully float inside.

Mission Control continues to monitor your vital signs as you go through the normal decompression routine. Finally they determine that you don't have a fever or sickness. Once the decompression is complete you check your suit thoroughly, but find nothing amiss. It must have been space motion sickness. But it doesn't matter now. Your spacewalk is over. Another astronaut can finish the repairs.

THE END

To follow another path, turn to page 11.
To read the conclusion, turn to page 101.

The pump is part of the station's cooling system. Ammonia is pumped through tubes around the station to absorb heat. Other systems remove the heat from the ammonia and release it into space. A broken pump means the system can't cool things down. There's no way to fix the pump from inside the station. The whole pump has to be replaced. Fortunately the station has extra pumps.

You and another crew member float out into space and slowly make your way to the broken pump using the special handrails that are installed along the outside of the ISS. It takes some time to get where you need to be, but you don't mind, since you have a great view of Earth below you. Finally you get to the broken pump.

Turn the page.

The pumps are about the size of a laundry dryer. You perch on the end of the robotic arm, and the two of you remove the broken unit.

All of this takes several hours, which means there isn't enough time to hook up the new pump. That will have to wait for the next spacewalk tomorrow. You accomplished what you needed to do today, so tomorrow's mission should go well. You gaze at Earth as you make your way back to the hatch, smiling at the best workplace view in the universe.

THE END

To follow another path, turn to page 11.
To read the conclusion, turn to page 101.

The Seeds In Space experiment started a few months ago, when schools in Germany, Russia and the Netherlands got kits of seeds. The idea is to compare the plants grown from those seeds with same seeds grown on the space station. The space seeds were grown in the dark and in the light.

Today you will be on a live video feed with the students at their schools. The cameras start and you say hello to all the kids on Earth. Then you all take a look at the space plants. The plants grown in the dark had grown in random directions. Plants in the light were green and healthy, and they'd all grown towards the light.

Turn the page.

"This tells us that plants need light and gravity to grow best," you say into the video monitor. "Light and gravity help the plants know which way to grow. If there's no light or gravity, the plants get confused."

When it's time to end, you wave to the camera. "If we ever go on long space missions to the Moon or Mars, we'll understand how to grow our own food," you say. "Thank you for being a part of this space experiment."

THE END

To follow another path, turn to page 11.
To read the conclusion, turn to page 101.

Your last job of the day is a fun one: taking pictures. For a long time the only window in the space station was the round one in the Destiny module. In 2010 a dome-shaped cupola was installed on the station. Its seven windows give astronauts and scientists a brilliant view of space and Earth. The experiment you're working on is called Crew Earth Observations. Crew members take photos and video of Earth as the station orbits the planet. Scientists will study these images to see how the Earth changes over time. They can also observe things like hurricanes, floods and volcanic eruptions.

Today your job is to take photos of cities at night. The space station orbits Earth every 92 minutes, so you fly over night-time Earth many times in your workday.

Turn the page.

In the middle of this task, you slowly lower the camera. Seeing the Sun rise over Earth is a spectacular thing. Often you forget to take pictures, and stare at Earth instead. You can't believe you're one of the few humans who get to see Earth from space.

Because of the speed at which the ISS orbits Earth, the crew sees 16 sunrises and sunsets each day.

THE END

To follow another path, turn to page 11.
To read the conclusion, turn to page 101.

The space station is designed to withstand space-junk impacts. There's the inner area where the astronauts live and work, then a layer of insulation. The outer shell is made of aluminium and Kevlar, the same material used to make bulletproof vests. Engineers tested this protective layer by shooting at it with high-powered guns. Still, even a tiny fleck of paint barrelling around in space could do a lot of damage if it hit the station.

Normally it takes about 30 hours to make the calculations for a move. Then it will take more time to move the station. But there's not enough time to do all that – the debris is only about six hours away.

Turn the page.

NASA and Mission Control monitor a specific area around the ISS. They call this area "the pizza box". This imaginary boundary is about 1.6 kilometres (1 mile) deep, 48.2 kilometres (30 miles) across, and 48.2 kilometres long. If anything looks like it's going to fly into the pizza box, they pay attention. This debris will fly well inside – only 4 kilometres (2 miles) from the station. It sounds like a long distance away. But for debris travelling at high speed, it's much too close for comfort.

The ground team will activate a four-minute "burn", firing the thrusters. This will move the space station a kilometre or so higher. You and the station crew don't have to do anything but wait.

In several hours the crew gets the "all clear" message. The move worked! The station is saved.

THE END

To follow another path, turn to page 11.
To read the conclusion, turn to page 101.

Everyone has gathered in front of a video camera so the president can see you. Then President Obama's voice says "Hello ISS, Obama here!" He greets the crew, then says, "I wanted to call and say how personally proud I am of you, and all that you're accomplishing. We're always inspired by images of you guys at work. You are setting such a great example with your dedication, courage, commitment to exploration. These are traits that built America and you guys personify them."

"Thank you, Mr. President," you say. "We're honoured."

THE END

To follow another path, turn to page 11.
To read the conclusion, turn to page 101.

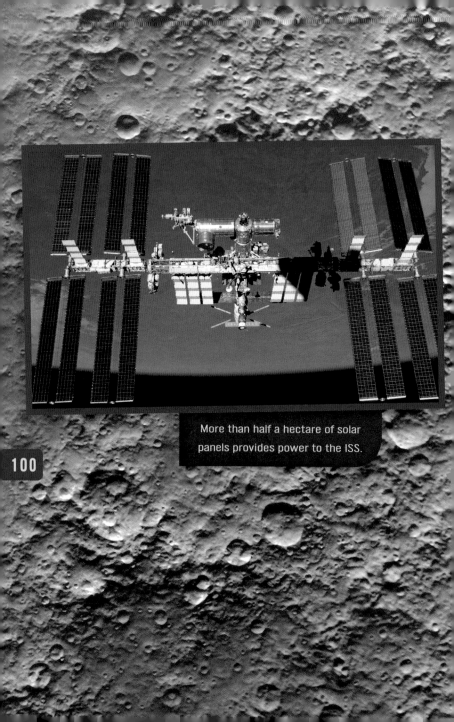

More than half a hectare of solar panels provides power to the ISS.

CHAPTER 5

LEGACY OF THE ISS

When President Ronald Reagan called for a new space exploration project in 1984, nothing like it had ever been designed and engineered before. The space station had to be tough enough to withstand the pressures of a high-speed launch and life in orbit. It also had to be lightweight, to be carried up into orbit easily. It took 14 years for the first piece of the International Space Station to go into orbit in 1998.

More than 200 people from 18 countries have visited the ISS. It took 115 spaceflights to construct the station, and astronauts have completed 193 spacewalks.

Some of the engineering designs that keep the International Space Station up and running are now used to help improve life on Earth. Many of the engineering feats used aboard ISS have helped advance important technologies on Earth.

The engineering technology in Canadarm and Canadarm2, the station's robotic arm, is used in robotic arms that assist in performing surgery. A small device astronauts use to measure nitric oxide in the space station's air can be helpful in diagnosing asthma. It can also help people with the disease to breathe more easily. The water recycling technology on the station is now used to bring clean water to remote areas of the world and to disaster victims during a crisis.

The ISS has another mission today, which is its biggest one yet: it is the foundation for NASA's Path to Mars programme. All of the ISS experiments on humans in space will help NASA understand how to create systems that let people live and work in space for even longer.

Engineers are using what they've learned about space transportation from the space shuttle and the ISS to develop new space vehicles that will travel further into space, and hopefully to Mars one day. Around 2019, NASA plans to launch a robotic mission to catch an asteroid, working from the technology developed for the ISS's robotic arm.

In the meantime, the ISS will be in orbit until at least 2024. In 2011 the U.S. Space Shuttle programme ended, but astronauts and cargo still travel to the ISS in spacecraft from other ISS-companion countries such as Russia and from commercial companies. While the United States is looking to Mars, other countries are already planning the next generation of space stations that will orbit Earth. The engineering and scientific breakthroughs of the ISS will live on in future space stations.

A SpaceX Dragon cargo craft approaches the ISS with a delivery. Dragon is the first commercial spacecraft to successfully attach to the station.

TIMELINE

1984 President Ronald Reagan announces that NASA will build an international space station

1998 The first sections of the ISS, the Russian module Zarya and the American module Unity, are launched

6 December 1998 The Zarya and Unity modules are connected to begin ISS construction

2 November 2000 The first space station crew arrives and stays for several months; the station has been continuously occupied ever since

10 February 2001 The laboratory module Destiny is installed on the ISS

22 April 2001 The CSA-built Canadarm2 robotic arm is installed on the ISS

2007 A shuttle crew delivers Harmony, a module for living and working, to the ISS

2008 The Columbus laboratory, developed by the European Space Agency (ESA), and the Kibo laboratory from Japan are added to the ISS

2009 Orbital debris threatens the ISS; crew members seek safety in the *Soyuz* "lifeboat"

February 2010 The ESA-built observatory module Cupola is installed

2015 Scott Kelly sets the record for the most cumulative days living in space by a NASA astronaut

2016 Scott Kelly returns safely to Earth

OTHER PATHS TO EXPLORE

In this book, you've seen how events from the past look different from three points of view. Perspectives on history are as varied as the people who lived it. Seeing history from many points of view is an important part of understanding it. Here are ideas for other International Space Station points of view to explore.

- President Reagan proposed the ISS at a time when many countries were at odds with one another. His call for international cooperation stunned many people around the world. How was the ISS project a good idea for the United States? What was the advantage of cooperating with other countries, instead of trying to beat them into space once again?

- The crew of the ISS spends much of its time conducting research and monitoring a large number of experiments. What are some of the ways that these experiments and research projects impact life on Earth? Refer to the text and outside sources for your answer.

FIND OUT MORE

Chris Hadfield and the International Space Station (Adventures in Space), Andrew Langley (Raintree, 2015).

Exploring the International Space Station (Searchlight Books: What's Amazing About Space?), Laura Hamilton Waxman (Lerner, 2015).

Ground Control to Major Tim: The Space Adventures of Major Tim Peake, Clive Gifford (Wayland, 2017).

WEBSITES

www.bbc.co.uk/guides/zyq4wxs
Film clips and photographs describe what life is like for astronauts on the International Space Station and what happens to the human body in space.

www.esa.int/esaKIDSen/SEMZXJWJD1E_ LifeinSpace_0.htm
This website has information and photographs from the European Space Agency about the International Space Station and living in space.

GLOSSARY

ammonia a colourless gas or liquid used for refrigeration and in cleaning products

astronaut a person who is trained to live and work in space

electrolysis the process of using an electric current to cause a chemical change

engineer a person who uses science and maths to plan, design or build

nitric oxide a colourless gas that is present in the atmosphere

orbit the path an object follows as it goes around the Sun or a planet

robotic of or relating to robots

satellite an object that moves around a planet or other cosmic body

tether to fasten by a line that limits range of movement

BIBLIOGRAPHY

Catchpole, John E. *The International Space Station: Building for the Future*. New York: Springer, 2008.

Harland, David M. and John E. Catchpole. *Creating the International Space Station*. New York: Springer, 2002.

"International Space Station." Boeing. April 28, 2016. http://www.boeing.com/space/international-space-station/.

"International Space Station." NASA. April 28, 2016. https://www.nasa.gov/mission_pages/station/main/index.html.

"International Space Station: Human Spaceflight and Exploration." ESA. April 28, 2016. http://www.esa.int/Our_Activities/Human_Spaceflight/International_Space_Station.

Kay, W. D. *Defining NASA: The Historical Debate over the Agency's Mission*. Albany, N.Y.: State University of New York Press, 2005.

Kitmacher, Gary. *Reference Guide to the International Space Station*. Washington, D.C.: National Aeronautics and Space Administration, 2010.

Sharp, Tim. "International Space Station: Facts, History & Tracking." Space.com. April 5, 2016. http://www.space.com/16748-international-space-station.html.

"Space Station Under Construction: Building a Ship Outside a Shipyard." NASA. April 28, 2016. http://www.nasa.gov/mission_pages/station/main/iss_construction.html.

INDEX